I0140535

CLEARING THE FOG

A JOURNEY TO TRUTH FAITH AND PURPOSE

BY

GEORGIE A MCKENZIE

Clearing the Fog

Copyright © 2025

by Georgie Mckenzie

DEDICATION

I wish to dedicate this book to my Lord Jesus Christ, the head of the church, and to the body of Christ, which is comprised of all believers around the world.

ACKNOWLEDGMENT

First and foremost, I give all honor and glory to my Lord and Savior, Jesus Christ. Thank You, Lord, for saving me, accepting me as your child, and placing the desire to write this book within me. Only through Your grace and love have I been able to embark on this journey, and I am forever grateful for Your guidance, mercy, and unchanging faithfulness.

I also wish to express my heartfelt gratitude to the prophet, whose name I will not mention, for being a vessel of truth and transformation in my life. Their bold and Spirit-led ministry profoundly awakened my understanding of serving a living and loving God. The prophet's impact has deepened my commitment to walking faithfully with the Lord and serving Him with intentionality and purpose.

Finally, I honor the memory of my late sister, Dorothy Higgs, a remarkable woman of faith who was one of my most incredible supporters. Dorothy was a constant source of encouragement and strength, always there when I needed someone to confide in. Her words of wisdom, often grounded in God's truth, lifted me during moments of doubt and discouragement. She reminded me of God's presence and call to remain steadfast in my journey. Dorothy's unwavering belief in God's promises inspires and guides me. I am profoundly grateful to God for the time I shared with her and the legacy of faith she left behind.

Contents

Introduction: A Life in the Fog

Most often, we go through life with our eyes open, yet we sometimes find it difficult to see and grasp even the simplest realities about our life, purpose, and existence. This is because open eyes do not necessarily guarantee sight and vision. From a scriptural perspective, we know it is possible to have our eyes wide open and still be blind to the realities all around us. Hence, Jesus referred to the Pharisees, Sadducees, and teachers of the law as "blind guides". Perhaps what is even more distressing is the fact that oftentimes we attempt to lead others even when it is obvious that we do not have a clear picture of the future ahead of us.

One of the dangers of driving through a fog is that we are prone to having an accidental collision with others. Perhaps the reason we often go through certain "accidental collisions" in life is that we spend most of our lives living in a societal fog. This explains why we do not see things from a scriptural perspective. It is almost impossible to see life from God's point of view when we are constantly blinded by the worldly fog that surrounds us daily.

The story of my life is the experience of one who has lived through the fog of the enemy until the light of God's Word gave me a new sense of purpose, vision, and direction. However, by the mercies of God, I now see with eyes opened the truth about life and the deception of the enemy.

I grew up the last child in a family of eleven children, a blessing in many ways but also a source of quiet loneliness. Being the youngest often meant being left to myself. My siblings, caught up in their own lives and struggles, didn't have much time for the little one at the end of the line. I spent countless hours alone, wandering through my thoughts, building a world within myself. This solitude shaped me into an introvert, someone who observed life more than participated in it.

i

We lived in the Bahamas, a land known for its beauty and vibrant culture—but beneath the sunshine, I often felt like a shadow. Christianity was the major religion there, and the church was woven into the fabric of our lives. Every Sunday, we dressed in our finest and filed into the sanctuary, the rhythm of the service familiar and comforting. Yet, even in this place of faith and community, I often felt like an outsider.

I heard the teachings of God's love, His grace, and His power. I heard about Jesus the Savior who gave His life for humanity. But I couldn't help questioning: "Who is this God? How could He love us so deeply, knowing all our flaws? Why did He create us knowing that our existence would always be a source of concern to Him?" These thoughts swirled in my mind, questions I dared not speak aloud for fear of judgment or misunderstanding.

As I grew older, I accepted Jesus as my Lord and Savior. I remember that moment clearly—the prayer, the commitment, and the hope that something would change. And yet, the questions didn't go away. I wanted to believe in this love I had been taught about, but I struggled to feel it. I longed to connect with others in the church, to find community among those who called themselves Christians. However, something always seemed to be missing. Conversations felt shallow, relationships distant, and I often felt like I didn't quite belong.

Even as I sang the hymns and prayed the prayers, I couldn't escape the fog that clouded my heart and mind. The faith I was raised in felt like an obligation, a tradition, rather than a personal connection to a living God. I wondered if I was the only one who felt this way, or if others were just better at hiding it. In my solitude, I sought answers. I read the Bible, trying to understand the depths of His love. I prayed, hoping for clarity. But the fog remained, leaving me to wrestle with my doubts and longings in silence.

Looking back, I see now that those early years were the foundation of my journey—a journey that would take me through the fog and into the light of truth. But at the time, I was just a quiet child, questioning, searching, and waiting for the moment when everything would finally make sense. Time passed, and my questions lingered. I wanted to find a reason—some undeniable truth—that explained why God loved us so deeply. My faith was there, but it felt incomplete as though I were holding pieces of a puzzle I couldn't quite put together.

Then Came the Turning Point

This feeling of emptiness went on for several years until I had a prophetic encounter that opened my eyes to the revelation of God's love. This experience changed my life forever. This was the beginning of the turning point in the fog. In November 2019, when I was about 46 years old, I attended a prophetic ministry in the Bahamas. It was an evening etched into my memory, one that would forever change the way I understood God and His love. I remember sitting on the balcony of the church, observing the congregation below. There was a sense of anticipation in the air as the prophet stepped forward, her presence commanding attention.

She didn't waste time. Her worship was focused, serious, and filled with a power that seemed to come from deep within. Most of the congregation, however, seemed more captivated by her than by the One she represented. They watched her; fascinated, but not engaged in the worship she called for. Sensing this, she stopped and asked a question that pierced the atmosphere—and my heart.

"Why are you watching me?" she demanded, her voice steady but full of emotion. "How do you serve a King? Is this how you would serve a King?"

Her words struck me like lightning. At that moment, it was as though a veil began to lift. I looked around, and I looked inward. Was I guilty of the same? Had I spent years going through the motions, more focused on the act of worship than the God I claimed to serve? Her question wasn't just directed at the congregation; it was directed at me.

From that night on, I began to truly question what it meant to be a Christian. I didn't just want to believe; I wanted to understand. I wanted to know why God's love for us was so great, and how I could serve Him in a way that honored Him as the King He is.

As I wrestled with these questions, I found myself drawn to the book of Genesis. One verse in particular stood out: "God created mankind in his image, in the image of God he created them; male and female he created them. " (Genesis 1:27)

And then it clicked. It was as though the Holy Spirit Himself whispered the meaning to me. We are made in the image of God—not just in form, but in essence, reflecting His love, creativity, and desire for relationship. This revelation opened my eyes to something profound: just as parents love their children unconditionally, so does God love us.

I thought about earthly parents, and how they represent God to their children. A parent's love is so deep that they would sacrifice anything for their child. Even when children turn their backs on their parents, the love remains, unwavering and unconditional. That's the kind of love God has for us—but multiplied way beyond what we could ever imagine.

I thought of the parable of the prodigal son, how the father welcomed his wayward child home with open arms, no questions asked. That's God. He sees us, flawed and broken, and loves us anyway. His love is greater than any earthly love we could experience or comprehend.

At that moment, the fog began to clear. I saw God not just as a distant Creator, but as a loving Father who cherishes His children. The idea we are His creation, made in His image, became more than a concept—it became the foundation of my faith. This revelation didn't just answer my questions; it completely transformed me. It gave me a new understanding of what it means to serve the Lord, not out of obligation, but out of love and gratitude for His endless, unimaginable love for us.

I have been living in the light of this revelation for several years now and it has made all the difference in my life. However, I know there are many believers out there who are still living in the fog even though they regularly participate in church activities. My goal is to help them see the light that I have seen so they can gain a better understanding of what it means to walk with God and worship Him in spirit and truth. Jesus said to the Samaritan woman at Jacob's well: "You worship whom you know not." Unfortunately, this seems to be the case with so many Christians in the body of Christ today.

Many believers have been blinded by a thick religious fog that prevents them from seeing and knowing God the Father, Jesus the Son, and the Holy Spirit. I know this to be true because I have been there. It brings to mind the Pharisees and Sadducees who pride themselves as the custodians of the laws of Moses and the temple of God but were blinded from seeing the truth about Jesus Christ.

A Prayer for the Reader

Dear Reader,

It is my humble prayer that as journey through the pages of this book, you will come to the realization and the consciousness of God's love for humanity that made Him sacrifice His precious son on the cross of Calvary. It is also my desire that you will come to the understanding of His love for you as His beloved child.

Although this book contains many stories about my personal experience, it is certainly not about me. I do not wish to be seen as a person who has attained perfection in my walk with God but instead, as one who is trying to help others overcome a common challenge that plagues us as believers in our journey to attaining perfection before God.

I earnestly pray that as you read this book, you will have an encounter with the love of God as I did several years ago. Our Christianity would remain a mere religion but for the encounters that we have. Jacob was destined to be great, having inherited the blessings of Abraham through Isaac his father. However, until he had an encounter with God, nothing changed. For many believers, nothing has changed even after they decided to follow Christ. However, there comes a turning point in every man's life where things begin to change and I am fully persuaded that this could be your moment.

It is therefore important for me to say that this book is more than just a retelling of my experiences; it is an invitation for you to explore the deeper truths about our existence and the immense love of a Creator who made us in His image. Together, we'll peel back the layers of illusion and uncover the reality of life—the meaning of who we are, why we are here, and how much we are cherished by the One who made us.

You can expect to find honest reflections, moments of clarity, and revelations that came to me in the fog of doubt and questioning. I'll share with you the turning points that opened my eyes and heart and helped me understand what it truly meant to serve the Lord and to embrace His love.

Whether you are wrestling with questions about God, seeking purpose, or simply curious about a life rooted in truth, this book will guide you on a journey of discovery. It is my hope and prayers that by the end, you too will see clearly how deeply loved and valued you are by the Creator of the universe.

This is not a perfect story, but it is a real one, written with the hope that my journey will inspire yours. My purpose is not to bring a message of condemnation or superiority but of inspiration and encouragement. There is hope for everyone who truly desires to see with their eyes opened- the truth about God beyond religious dogmas and assumptions. Christ has come to show us the way, to reveal the truth, and to give us life. Therefore, no more would we walk in darkness or be blinded by the fog.

Come with me and let us walk this path together, hand in hand, as we seek truth, light, and the everlasting love of our Heavenly Father.

With gratitude and hope,

Georgie A Mckenzie

Chapter One

The Illusion and Vanity of This World

When our eyes are opened, it becomes easy to see that the world is full of nothing but illusions and vanities. Most of the things that are highly regarded in our world today are of no eternal value. This is why the scriptures tell us; "…For what is highly esteemed among men is an abomination in the sight of God." (Lk. 16:15). It is sad to see that even preachers who ought to be leading others to the Kingdom of God are themselves engrossed in the pursuit of the illusions and material vanities of the world. There needs to be a reawakening of the consciousness of spiritual realities in the body of Christ.

1.1 Worldly Distractions: Materialism, Media, and the Pursuit of Success

Perhaps the church is no longer making spiritual progress because we are constantly being distracted by the things of the world. So much distraction exists in every direction that it seems impossible to focus on spiritual realities. Most often, we are distracted by things that are not scripturally wrong or sinful but are of no eternal value to us. For example, watching the Television is not a sinful act but it could hinder our spiritual progress if not curtailed. We need to understand that the value system of this world is constantly at variance with the principles and ideologies of God. This is why the scripture warns us; "…Do you not know that friendship with the world is enmity with God? Whoever therefore wants to be a friend of the world makes himself an enemy of God." (Jam. 4:4). We cannot make spiritual progress as long as we are being distracted by the mundane illusions and vanities of this world.

The world is focused on materialism with little or no regard for genuine spirituality. Wealth, fame, beauty, power, and vain success are the only things that seem to matter to the people of this world. Unfortunately,

1

these are fast becoming the standard and focus of some Christians in the church. We have abandoned the supernatural in pursuit of the superficial and shifted our gaze from that which is eternal because of temporary distractions in our society.

Even the world's definition of success is nothing but vanity compared to the true biblical meaning of success. The Rich fool in the parable of Jesus thought he had everything in life and considered himself a highly successful person having accumulated so much wealth until it became apparent that he was nothing but a failure in the sight of God. The Apostle Paul on the other hand is highly regarded as one of the most successful men that ever lived on the face of the earth, even though he never lived in wealth and affluence. Several centuries after the death of this great apostle, his works and impacts are still visible on the earth touching generations and millions of lives.

We must never be distracted by the pursuit of worldly success because its allure is only temporal. You may not have all the money in the world but if you are living out heaven's purpose for your life, believe me, you are a success in the eyes of God. True and biblical success can only be found when we discover the purpose for which we were created and begin to fulfill it. Consider our Lord Jesus Christ for example. His purpose and mission on earth as assigned by God the Father was the redemption of the human race. When Jesus hung on the cross naked, in pain and agony, he was mocked for his failure to save himself after performing so many miraculous signs and wonders in the course of his earthly ministry.

Although Jesus died as a failure in the eyes of all men, in the eyes of God he was a success because he fulfilled the exact purpose for which he came into the world. You see my friend; we can never be accurate as long as we keep measuring ourselves according to the standard of this world. It is time to set aside worldly distractions and return to the ways of God.

The future of Christianity is in danger today because young people who ought to be on fire for God are being distracted daily by entertainment, television programs, and social media. The average Christian teen and young adult today has to deal with high levels of distractions that those in previous generations never had to deal with. With so many social media and entertainment applications such as Facebook, Instagram, YouTube, TikTok, and several others, on our mobile devices, we are just a click away from worldly distractions. Consequently, we no longer have time for basic Christian activities such as praying, studying, meditating, and seeking God. Teens and young believers are now more interested in getting more likes and followers on social media than in genuine soul-lifting fellowship with other believers.

Christian families no longer enjoy conversations and fellowships and have very little or no time for family devotions. Most often, family members begin each day by scrolling through their phones instead of having a quiet time alone with God. Even at meal times, each one seems lost in their devices and this makes it difficult for them to engage in meaningful spiritual conversations.

There are two things we need to understand about the worldly distractions that constantly surround us. Firstly, distractions come to us with a singular intent, which is to stop us from reaching our goal. They are neither accidental nor do they come to us coincidentally. It should be of no surprise to us that as we approach the end of the world and the time of the second coming of Christ, there seems to be a surge in the level of distractions in the world around us. Secondly, underneath the noise of societal distractions lies nothing but a barren emptiness. Just as the old saying goes: "Empty vessels make the loudest noise." Solomon the wisest king that ever lived on the face of the earth puts it perfectly; "…Vanity of vanities, all is vanity." (Ecc. 1:2).

1.2   The Impact of Cultural and Societal Norms on Our Beliefs and Priorities

We live in a world that is dominated by cultural norms. These norms have been in existence for several decades before we were born. More often than not we live according to these norms hence they influence our belief system. However, the scripture warns us against yielding to these societal and cultural norms when it says: "And do not be conformed to this world, but be transformed by the renewing of your mind, that you may prove what is that good and acceptable and perfect will of God." (Rom. 12:2). The reason the scripture warns us against these norms is because they have a way of negatively influencing our thoughts, actions, and perception of life in general.

As believers, we ought to pattern our lives according to scriptural principles and not after the standards of this world. This is because the world is in a fallen state and this has been the case ever since Adam and Eve transgressed the commandment of God in Eden. Perhaps one reason why it is often so difficult to break free from cultural norms is that these norms have been a part of our lifestyle from a tender age. And even after accepting Christ, they continue to influence us subtly. Growing up, we absorbed these norms unconsciously, whether as a part of family tradition or the educational system. They have now become our standard for determining what is wrong or right.

There is so much pressure on us to conform to societal norms even though these norms are against scriptural standards and principles. For instance, in our society today, lesbianism, gay relationships, and same-sex marriages are fast becoming acceptable norms. Churches and believers are constantly being pressured to conform to these norms even though they are contrary to the laws of God.

Right from the Bible days, the church has always been under pressure to live according to the dictates of the traditions and culture of society. Even after the coming of Christ and the outpouring of the Holy Spirit on the day of Pentecost, the early believers still held onto the traditions of circumcision and the law of Moses. This became a source of dispute in the early church when the Christian Jews tried to impose the tradition of circumcision and the law of Moses on the Gentile converts who had accepted Christ. Paul who was a Jew but also an apostle to the Gentiles vehemently opposed this.

Hence, he wrote to the church in Galatia: "For in Christ Jesus neither circumcision nor uncircumcision avails anything, but faith working through love" (Gal. 5:6). When we allow traditional and cultural norms to influence

4

us, not only do we short-change ourselves from receiving the full benefits and blessing of redemption, but we also become a hindrance to the salvation and faith of others.

Man was created as a free moral agent capable of making his choices and decisions. This also gives us the power to make and effect the changes we want. We might not be able to change the worldview of society or the culture and tradition around us but we can decide whether or not we want to live by these standards. We can also choose to break free from inherited cultural norms that are contrary to biblical standards and principles. It's all a matter of choice and decision. The Bible tells us about the story of four Hebrew boys: Daniel, Shadrach, Meshach, and Abednego, who decided not to live by the existing customs and traditions in Babylon even though they were captives in the land. Not only did they refuse to defile themselves with the land's cultural delicacy but they also disregarded the traditional norm of bowing to idols. The actions of these Hebrew youths should serve as a source of inspiration to us.

While it is true that growing up with these norms makes it difficult to change, a transformation is not entirely impossible. We however need to identify these norms and recognize their influence. Perhaps herein lies the challenge, because we have lived with these norms for quite a very long time, it is often challenging to identify them because some of them have become a cognitive part of our behavior by default.

The key to breaking free from every form of societal norm is the Word of God. Firstly, just as the scripture admonished us in the book of Romans chapter 12 vs 2; we must be determined not to conform to the ways and patterns of this world. There is no doubt that our refusal to conform to societal norms would attract a lot of criticism from those around us. As a matter of fact, some of our friends could become our foes simply because we chose to walk along a different path. Secondly, we have to be transformed by renewing our minds with the Word of God. We need to understand that becoming a New Creation through salvation does not guarantee a renewed mindset.

5

When we receive Christ and become born again, we only experience a rebirth of our spirit man. However, our minds and bodies remain the same. You see, over the years, our minds have been programmed by societal norms and traditions and this has affected our thinking, attitude, and behavior. Hence, we would need to completely renew our mindset to break free from the strongholds previously formed in our minds. This mental transformation is only possible when we meditate on the Word of God.

1.3 My Experience of Living Under Worldly Illusions

For much of my life, my relationship with God felt distant—more like an idea than a reality. I believed in Him, attended church regularly, and followed the motions of faith. But deep down, I often felt disconnected. My prayers were spoken more out of habit than a sense of connection, and my worship felt more like a duty than a heartfelt expression of love.

I lived within an illusion—a world where God existed, but not fully in my heart. I thought that by following the routines of faith, I was doing enough. I attended services, sang the hymns, and recited the scriptures. Yet, I often found myself questioning who God truly was and why His love was so significant. I wanted to believe in the profound truths I was taught, but they often seemed just out of reach like a light I couldn't quite touch.

Looking back, I see how the distractions of the world played a role in this illusion. Society's values—success, material wealth, and external validation—often overshadowed the spiritual truths I longed to embrace. I found myself chasing goals and achievements, thinking they would bring me closer to a sense of purpose. But no matter how much I accomplished, that inner emptiness remained.

Even in church, where faith should be at its strongest, I felt disconnected. I struggled to find community, often feeling like an outsider among those who called themselves Christians. Conversations seemed surface-level, and the warmth I longed for in relationships was absent. I wondered if my doubts and questions made me unworthy, or if I was simply missing something that others had found.

I accepted Jesus as my Lord and Savior, hoping that act alone would bridge the gap I felt. And while it was an important step, my questions didn't vanish. I still wrestled with understanding His love, His grace, and His purpose for my life. I couldn't grasp why a perfect God would care so deeply for someone as flawed as me.

The illusion was that I thought I knew God, but I had only scratched the surface. I was living a faith that was more about appearances than transformation, more about tradition than relationship. My heart longed for something deeper, but I didn't know how to break through the fog that surrounded me.

It wasn't until I began to question, to truly seek answers, that the illusion started to fade. I realized God wasn't distant or indifferent; I had been the one keeping Him at arm's length. He had been there all along, patiently waiting for me to open my heart and invite Him in fully.

This realization marked the beginning of a profound transformation in my faith. I started to understand that a relationship with God isn't about perfection or rituals—it's about surrender, trust, and love. The journey out of the illusion wasn't easy, but it was worth every step, leading me closer to the truth of who God is and the life He desires for us to live.

I am forever grateful to God that I no longer live under the shadow of worldly illusions as I so often did in the past. Rather with eyes open, I now see beyond the temporary vanities of life as I gaze on the realities of eternal spiritual truths.

Chapter Two

Understanding the True Meaning of Life

So often we try so hard to understand the true meaning of life. Over the years, the greatest of philosophers and scholars have attempted to present an accurate definition of the meaning of life and human existence.

What the world has failed to realize is that the true meaning of life is not found in a theoretical definition but in a person. The Bible records that Jesus said to Thomas: "I am the way, the truth, and the life. No one comes to the Father except through Me." (Jh. 14:6). To truly understand life, we have to get acquainted with the one from whom life itself originated.

The Bible tells us that in the beginning, God created both the heavens and the earth. The material from which He made the Universe and all life in it is His Word. This is why the scripture tells us concerning Jesus: "All things were made through Him, and without Him, nothing was made that was made." (Jh. 1:3). Jesus is the Word of God and he is the source of life and getting to know him is the first step to understanding the fundamentals of life.

Not only do we need to get acquainted with the living Word in the person of Christ, but we also need a good understanding of the written Word in the Bible to enhance our knowledge and understanding of the concept of life. Those who attempt to find the true meaning of life outside of Christ and the Word will only find frustration, emptiness, and vanity. Perhaps this explains why some people never find fulfillment in life despite their accomplishments and material possessions.

8

Man was never meant to live without God. The first man God created maintained continuous fellowship with Him in Eden and when the fellowship was broken through sin, all that was left was nakedness and emptiness. When Adam and Eve ate the fruit from the tree of Knowledge of good and evil, their eyes were opened to see the truth of the vanity of life outside God and His Word.

2.1 Exploring Ancient Wisdom and Scriptural Truths

To get a good understanding of life we must seek the wisdom of the old because there is nothing new under the sun. This ancient wisdom can only be found in the pages of the scriptures. We need to understand that wisdom is the principal thing in life (Prov. 4:7). Without ancient wisdom, we cannot fully comprehend the dynamics of life. Ancient wisdom consists of timeless precepts and principles that are relevant and applicable in the modern era.

It is amazing to see people treat the Bible as an outdated book containing irrelevant information when in reality, it is the most relevant book on the face of the earth. The Word of God is divine wisdom for all generations. Ever since the Bible became available in print, every generation has found it relevant and applicable to their day and time.

Taking a personal journey through the pages of the scriptures was how I began my exploration of this ancient wisdom. I began this journey from the book of Genesis and I was fascinated by the creation story because it offered me a glimpse into the intentionality of life. I was enraptured at the fact that "God created man in His own image." I meditated on this phrase as it reverberated deep within my soul. This opened my eyes to see God's purpose for me and the entire human race. I also saw that just as the scriptures stated, we were wonderfully and fearfully made (Ps. 139:14). We are not some random creatures that came out of scientific or natural evolutions rather we were made after the very likeness of God.

As I journeyed further through the scriptures, I marveled at the wisdom in the words of the prophets and the parables of Jesus. One parable in particular stood out; the story of the prodigal son. This story depicted the everlasting love of God towards us. It doesn't matter how far or how long we have been away from God; He is ever willing to receive and restore us to fellowship with Him. The story of the prodigal son reveals that God is a loving and kind-hearted Father whose love for His children is unconditional, forgiving, and steadfast.

Going through the psalms and proverbs was such a wonderful experience for me. The psalms for instance fill us with so much hope and comfort and teach us that we are not alone in our struggles. The psalms also encourage us to cry to God in our times of distress and to hold onto Him even in the darkest moments of our lives. I found the book of proverbs most of which were written by Solomon the wisest of kings to be a treasured bank of wisdom. The book of proverbs much like the Ecclesiastes calls for us to think about our way of life and encourages us to choose wisdom over folly.

In all my study and exploration, I discovered that the Bible contains the ancient wisdom that we need to lead successful lives. The wisdom contained in the pages of the scriptures would help us find peace, success, and joy in all endeavors of life. This scriptural wisdom teaches us to live in peace, love, forgiveness, and harmony with others, letting go of pride, hurts, and offenses.

Perhaps the distinguishing factor between the Bible and other books is that it not only offers information to the mind but also guarantees the transformation of the Soul. Through the guidance of scriptural wisdom, we can develop a solid relationship with God and others around us. As a matter of fact, this ancient wisdom teaches us that the most important thing in life is to love the Lord and also to love your neighbor as yourself (Matt. 22:37). We can never go wrong in life when we walk in love and wisdom.

Until we embrace the ancient wisdom found in the scriptures, we will never understand what true spirituality is all about. In my study and exploration, I discovered a depth of spirituality that is far beyond what the world could ever offer. Life is far deeper than the physical, there is a spiritual dimension of life that is only accessible through scriptural wisdom. Most often, we live under the illusion that life is all about acquiring material wealth and possession. However, the ancient wisdom of scriptures tells us:

"For what will it profit a man if he gains the whole world, and loses his own soul? [37] Or what will a man give in exchange for his soul?" (Mk 8:36-37). Embracing the ancient wisdom found in scriptures would open our eyes to see that the true meaning of life is not found in the pursuit and acquisition of temporary possessions but in developing a spiritual walk with God-the source of all life.

2.2 The Purpose of Our Existence: Love, Connection, and Higher Calling

The purpose of our existence has always been a source of debate and deliberation for several years and perhaps generations. A common question in the mind of many young people is "Why am I here on Earth? What is the reason for my existence in the world?" I found the answers to these questions in my explorative journey through the scriptures. By connecting with the ancient wisdom found in the Word of God, I discovered that the purpose of our existence is established on three scriptural principles; love, connection, and a higher calling. Let's examine these three powerful interconnected principles one after the other.

1. Love-The Foundation of Our Being: We can never understand the purpose of our existence unless we learn what it means to live in love. Most often, we erroneously presume love to mean emotional feelings when in reality it is the foundation of our being because the scriptures tell us that God is love and we were made in His image and likeness. We can never miss our purpose as long as our actions are motivated by love. Jesus was motivated by his love for us and he fulfilled his purpose and mission on earth. He laid down the perfect example for us to follow in the discovery and pursuit of our purpose. Love should always motivate us with the desire to serve and be a blessing to others and this is what purpose is essentially about. Every one of us has a purpose on earth to serve God and humanity in so many ways. And we can only do this successfully when we love God and our neighbors as we love ourselves.

2. Connection-Living in Relationship: Just as the old saying goes "No man is an Island." We all need one another because we were never meant to live in isolation. Shortly after He made man, God

11

pronounced everything to be good except for one thing: "...It is not good that man should be alone..." (Gen. 2:18). The scripture tells us further: "...But woe to him who is alone when he falls, for he has no one to help him up." (Ecc.4:10). Life becomes meaningful and purposeful through connection. We were made to connect one way or another- through family, friendship, community, or church and each connection offers strength, encouragement, support, and protection. The reason many people often do not see the need to connect with others is that they do not understand that human relationships are not perfect and often require vulnerability, forgiveness, and a willingness to serve others. Establishing relationships through connections offers us the opportunity both to demonstrate God's love to others and walk in the fullness of our calling and purpose.

3. A Higher Calling-Living with Purpose: Every believer has a calling and a purpose to fulfill. Walking in love and establishing relationships with others gives us the foundation for the fulfillment of our calling. Every one of us has been called and mandated with the task of carrying the good news to the ends of the earth. Jesus did not commit the Great Commission to apostles, prophets, evangelists, pastors, and teachers alone but to the entire body of believers. Irrespective of our various professions or vocation in society, we are required to use our gifts, experiences, talents, offices, and positions to serve others while also sharing the gospel with them. Living with a higher calling call for absolute surrender to the will of God. When we submit to the will of God, it becomes easy for Him to use us for His glory.

My perspective about life took a different turn when I discovered the purpose of our existence is rooted in the three aforementioned principles. I was no longer interested in following societal norms or conforming to the cultural standards of the world. Rather I made up my mind to live intentionally and see every day as an opportunity to demonstrate the love of God, establish a genuinely meaningful relationship with others, and walk in the path of my higher calling.

To me, purpose is not a burden but rather a gift freely given to every one of us. This is why I believe that we are neither here by accident nor by coincidence. We have been designed at such a time as this to fulfill a specific purpose in the agenda of God. And as we fulfill the purpose of God's higher calling, we will find a sense of peace and joy that is beyond description. At the end of our life on earth, just as Apostle Paul did, we would be able to declare boldly: "I have fought the good fight, I have finished the race, I have kept the faith." (2 Tim. 4:7).

2.3 My Journey to Understanding Life's True Meaning

Life has a way of unfolding slowly, like the turning of pages in a story. For many years, I walked through life with questions burning in my heart: *Why am I here? What is the purpose of all this?* I sought answers in the routines of daily life, the traditions of faith, and the fleeting joys of success, but nothing seemed to fully satisfy the ache within me. It was a journey—long, winding, and at times painful—but it led me to a truth that changed everything.

For much of my life, I had lived according to what the world defined as important: achieving goals, gaining acceptance, and following a prescribed path. I believed that if I checked off the right boxes, I would find fulfillment. Yet, despite these efforts, there was always a lingering sense of emptiness as if something crucial was missing.

My faith was present but shallow. I knew about God, attended church, and believed in the teachings I had grown up with, but my relationship with Him felt distant. I often questioned His love and purpose for my life. Why would an all-powerful Creator care about someone as ordinary as me? These doubts lingered in my heart, keeping me from fully embracing the faith I claimed to follow.

The turning point came during a moment of worship in a prophetic ministry. From that moment, I began to seek God with a new sense of urgency and sincerity. I turned to the Bible, not as a ritual but as a source of answers. I started with Genesis, where the profound truth that we are made in

13

God's image began to reshape my understanding of life. To be made in His image meant that my existence was intentional, filled with purpose and love.

I reflected on the love of a parent for their child—the kind of love that remains steadfast even when the child makes mistakes or turns away. This parallel helped me grasp why God's love for us is so profound and unchanging. We are His children, His creation, and His love is not dependent on our perfection but on His nature.

As I explored these truths, the meaning of life became clearer. Life is not about accumulating achievements, pleasing others, or following societal norms. Instead, it is about love—receiving God's love, reflecting it in how we treat others, and living in a way that glorifies Him. It is about connection—building relationships that bring joy, healing, and growth. And it is about purpose—using the gifts and opportunities God has given us to make a difference in the world.

This journey to understanding life's true meaning was not an instant revelation but a gradual unfolding of truth. It required me to let go of the distractions and illusions that had clouded my vision and to embrace a faith that was real, deep, and transformative.

Now, I see life with eyes opened as a precious gift, filled with opportunities to love, serve, and grow. The questions that once haunted me have become stepping stones to a deeper faith and a clearer understanding of my place in God's plan. And with each step I take, I am reminded that life's true meaning is not something we create—it is something we discover when we surrender to the One who created us.

Chapter Three

Overcoming the Enemies' Deception

One of the things I learned early in my journey to understanding the true meaning and purpose of life is that the enemy is constantly working to keep us from discovering the truth that leads to the joy, peace, and freedom God intended for us to experience. Most often, it is difficult for us to discern the works of the enemy because they are often subtle and deceptive. The church needs to learn to stand strong against the deception of the enemy because, in these last days, there would be an increase in the enemy's deception.

The Merriam-Webster dictionary refers to deception as the act of causing someone to accept as true or valid what is false. Deception started in the Garden of Eden where Adam and Eve were both misled into eating the fruit from the forbidden tree with the hope that they would not die but rather would be like God knowing good and evil.

Perhaps the reason why deception is so difficult to discern is that it often involves a combination of validity and falsehood. In deception, the enemy presents what is valid with the intention of luring us into falsehood. One of the ways through which we can overcome deception is by the complete and accurate knowledge of the truth of God's Word concerning every facet of our lives.

Although the enemy usually operates subtly and cunningly when attempting to carry out deception, through deep reflection, I have been able to identify some of the ways through which he operates, which include: spiritual forces, societal systems, and personal doubts.

15

3.1 Identifying the Enemy: Internal and External Enemies

We must learn to identify the enemy behind every attack. Knowing the enemy is a vital strategy that secures victory in warfare. Based on their mode of operations, we can categorize the enemy into two; internal and external enemies.

The external enemies are outside forces that are manipulated to work against us. These include negative spiritual forces and societal systems, just to name a few. These adversaries work against us by trying to get us to bow to the systems of the world.

On the other hand, we have so-called internal enemies because, unlike external enemies, these are forces that are resident within us. They include fear, self-doubt, and low self-esteem among several others.

Although both sets of enemies are dangerous, the internal forces are usually more difficult to discern and deal with in contrast to the external ones. And most often, it is the internal enemies and not the external forces that are likely to defeat us. Let us take a look at these two forces in greater detail.

3.2 Dealing with External Enemies: Spiritual Forces; Worldly and Societal Systems

As earlier established, the external forces we have to deal with can broadly be classified into two. Firstly, we have the spiritual forces that are behind the spiritual and invisible battles around us. Many believers are ignorant of the existence of these forces while others try to play down their existence and influence. However, regarding our confrontation with these enemies, the scripture warns us, "For we do not wrestle against flesh and blood, but against principalities, against powers, against the rulers of the darkness of this age, against spiritual hosts of wickedness in the heavenly places." (Eph. 6:12).

16

The fact these forces are invisible does not mean that they are non-existent. These enemies are constantly at work and most often their primary mission is to lure us into temptation, distract our attention from the Word of God, and eventually lead us down the path of disobedience and rebellion against God.

In times of difficulties and challenges, these spiritual forces often attempt to make us doubt and question the love of God by bombarding our minds with fearful and worrisome thoughts. I once experienced this in moments of doubt when the enemy whispered that my questions about God's love and purpose were proof of a weak faith. However, the moment I discerned these thoughts were a part of the enemy's ploy to pull me down, I quickly resisted them. We must never surrender to these spiritual forces rather we must be determined to resist them until victory is secured.

The second external enemy that we have to contend with is the societal system with its culture of distraction. We need to understand that the enemy is currently in charge of the affairs of this world. This is why the scriptures tell us not to love the things of the world. The scripture further tells us, "For all that is in the world—the lust of the flesh, the lust of the eyes, and the pride of life—is not of the Father but is of the world" (1 John 2:16). As earlier established, the things of the world are mere distractions that aim to hinder from running the race the God had ordained for us before the foundation of the world.

Unfortunately, I was trapped in the worthless pursuit of worldly success for several years only to find out how vain and hollow they were. This forced me to retreat and question my pursuit of these mundane and temporary values. With eyes opened, I realized I had gotten my priorities all wrong and this had negatively impacted my relationship with God. I had to retrace my steps and prioritize my relationship with God above everything else, and I am glad that I did.

17

3.3 Dealing with the Enemies Within: Self-Doubts and Negativity

The enemy within is difficult to deal with because they are often the product of our flaws and weaknesses. Chief amongst these internal enemies is our self-doubt. These doubts usually spring from deep within and often render us incapacitated and impotent in critical moments of our lives.

Our self-doubt is often a massive weapon in the hands of the enemy. In other words, by harboring these personal doubts within ourselves, we have placed a sword in the hand of the enemy with which he can hurt us. The same could be said about negativity and low self-esteem.

The enemy knows how to skillfully use the weapon of doubt against us. By amplifying our weaknesses, failures, and shortcomings he tries to intimidate us into thinking that we are not strong enough whereas our strength comes from God. The biggest hindrance to our faith in God is the doubts within us.

3.4 Recognizing the Enemy's Strategy of Deception

We need to learn to discern the enemy and his strategies early enough to minimize the damaging effects of his attacks. Being able to identify the enemy was an important step in my journey because it made me see the attacks as a part of his grand scheme against my soul and the purpose of my existence. Recognizing the enemy on time helps us prepare for the anticipated attacks by spending time in prayer, Bible study, and developing our relationship with God.

When dealing with the enemy's deception, we need to keep in mind three major tools are strategically used to perpetuate the nefarious acts of deception. These are fear, division, and lies. For clarity, we need to examine these three in greater detail.

1. Fear: Perhaps this is one of the deadliest tools often deployed against us by the adversary. According to the scriptures, fear is a spirit that is not from God (2 Tim. 1:7). It is often described as the enemy's

weapon of paralysis because it can stop us in our tracks if we give in to it. Fear has a voice that constantly lies to us. It is a voice that whispers to us that we cannot make it because we do not have what it takes to be successful. We must never believe the voice of fear because it speaks nothing but lies. For several years I was held back by my fears to the point where I found it difficult to trust God. I was afraid to take steps of faith because I was constantly held back by the fears in my heart. However, it wasn't long before I found out that the key to conquering fear was the Word of God. When we confront our fears with the Word, we are assured of victory.

2. Division: Such is the power of unity that the Bible tells us "Every Kingdom divided against itself is brought to desolation, and every city or house divided against itself will not stand" (Matt. 12:25). Even the enemy is aware of the destructive powers of division for the scripture tells us, "If Satan casts out Satan, he is divided against himself. How then will his Kingdom stand?" (Matt. 12:26). This is why he often uses division as a weapon against families, friendship, relationship, communities, and churches. The enemy knows that we are stronger together and often uses division as a strategy to weaken us. Perhaps one of the reasons why the body of Christ is weakened today is because we have fallen victim to the enemy's strategy of division. God wants the church united as one body in Christ knowing that unity and love are both instrumental for the fulfillment of His purposes on earth.

3. Lies: The enemy specializes in fabricating and spreading lies. Hence, he is referred to as the father of lies (Jh.8:44). Lies are the foundation of deception. The enemy often spreads lies that seem logical to our reasoning to fill our hearts and minds with fears. I know firsthand how devastating the enemy's lies can be because for years I believed in the lies of the enemies about my personality, weaknesses, and mistakes. And these lies kept me in a state of guilt and shame for a long time. However, I discovered the secret to overcoming the lies of the adversary is the Word of God. By meditating and immersing ourselves in God's Word, we can break free from the lies of the

enemy. This is why the scripture tells us, "And you shall know the truth, and the truth shall make you free." (Jh. 8:32).

Not only do we need to break free from the lies of the enemies but also from his other deceptive strategies such as fear and division. However, if we will be successful in doing this we need to get acquainted with the weapons of our warfare. The reason why many believers often become victims of the enemy's attack is that they are ignorant of the weapons at their disposal. The truth is that our weapons are far superior to those of the enemy. Hence the scripture tells us; "For the weapons of our warfare are not carnal but mighty in God for pulling down strongholds" (2 Corin.10:4). One of the most potent weapons of our warfare is the Word of God. It is a weapon that is sharper than any double-edged sword on the face of the earth (Heb. 4:12). Another weapon that is capable of pulling down the enemy's stronghold is prayer. When Jesus fasted for 40 days and nights in the wilderness and the enemy attempted to derail him, he overcame by declaring the Word that was written. I believe that if we properly engage the weapons of our warfare, we will successfully overcome the enemy and his deceptive strategies.

3.5 My Personal Experience with the Enemy's Influence

The enemy's influence often manifests in deeply personal ways, targeting our weaknesses, insecurities, and fears. These battles are not always visible to others; they are internal struggles that challenge our faith, distort our perceptions, and attempt to distance us from God's truth and love. My journey has been marked by these battles, moments when I wrestled with doubt, fear, and the lies that the enemy whispered into my mind.

One of my earliest and most persistent battles was with self-doubt. The enemy had a way of magnifying my flaws, convincing me that I wasn't good enough—not for people, not for opportunities, and certainly not for God. Every mistake I made became evidence in a mental case against me, and I began to see myself as unworthy of love or grace.

Fear was another weapon the enemy used against me. Whether it was fear of failure, fear of rejection, or fear of the unknown, it often kept me from stepping into the plans God had for my life. I would feel God's call to move forward, but fear would paralyze me, whispering that I wasn't ready, that I would fail, or that it wasn't worth the risk. It took me years to realize that fear was not from God, but a tool of the enemy to keep me from walking in faith.

Another personal battle was with distractions. The enemy used the busyness of life, the allure of material success, and the opinions of others to pull my focus away from God. I would find myself striving to meet societal expectations, chasing after achievements that the world deemed valuable but left me feeling empty. In doing so, I neglected my spiritual growth and often felt distant from God.

Even in my spiritual life, the enemy's influence would creep in. There were times when prayer felt like a chore, and reading the Bible felt like an obligation. The enemy would use these moments to convince me that my faith wasn't genuine, that I was failing as a Christian, and that God was disappointed in me. These thoughts created a cycle of guilt and shame, further distancing me from the relationship with God that I longed for.

Over time, as my eyes opened, I began to recognize the enemy's tactics for what they were: deliberate attempts to undermine my faith and keep me from living in God's truth. Through prayer, scripture, and the guidance of the Holy Spirit, I started to fight back. When fear crept in, I reminded myself of God's promises, like in Isaiah 41:10: *"Do not fear, for I am with you."* When self-doubt tried to take over, I turned to verses like Psalm 139:14: *"I am fearfully and wonderfully made."* When distractions threatened to consume me, I realigned my priorities by seeking God first.

These battles are ongoing, but each victory strengthens my faith and brings me closer to God. I've learned that while the enemy's influence is real, it is not greater than the power of God. The struggles I face are not a sign of weakness but an opportunity to grow in faith, to lean on God's strength, and to experience His grace in new ways.

21

Through these personal battles, I've come to understand that the enemy's influence is not the final word. God's truth, love, and power are greater than any lie, fear, or distraction. And with Him by my side, I can stand firm, even in the face of the enemy's strongest attacks.

Chapter Four

Breaking Free from the Dogmas of Worldly Illusions

Although the enemy's plan is to keep us from knowing the truth, a time comes when we eventually break free from the dogmas that have bound us. There are moments in our lives when the yokes finally break, the burdens are suddenly lifted, the veil is torn wide open, and the enemy's stronghold begins to crumble. These are profound moments that tend to make all the difference in our lives.

4.1 Key Realizations That Shattered My Illusions

Personally, there were key realizations that helped me shatter the illusions that held me down for so long. These realizations allowed me to see my life and purpose from God's perspective. Let me walk you through these realizations;

1. My worth comes from God and not the world: For several years, I measured my value by worldly standards: achievements, appearances, and the opinions of others. I believed I would finally feel fulfilled if I could meet these expectations. But no matter how much I accomplished or how hard I worked, the emptiness remained. However, the turning point came when I read Psalm 139:14 which says, "I am fearfully and wonderfully made." These words struck a chord deep within me. They reminded me that my worth isn't tied to what I do but to who I am—a creation of God, loved unconditionally. This realization shattered the illusion that I needed the world's approval and freed me to embrace the truth of my God-given identity.
2. God's love is unconditional: I often wrestled with the idea of God's love. I thought I had to earn through it good deeds, perfect faith, or unwavering devotion. But as I delved into scripture, I encountered verses like Romans 5:8 which tells us: "But God demonstrates his

own love for us in this: While we were still sinners, Christ died for us." It was a humbling realization: God's love doesn't depend on my performance. He loves me not because of who I am, but because of who He is. This truth shattered the illusion that I had to strive for His acceptance and replaced it with the peace of knowing that His love is a gift I can never earn or lose.

3. Life's Purpose is rooted in God's plan: For much of my life, I chased after what the world told me was important: success, recognition, and security. I believed achieving these things would make my life meaningful. But the more I pursued them, the more I realized how fleeting and hollow they were. The breakthrough came when I truly embraced Jeremiah 29:11: "For I know the plans I have for you," declares the Lord, "plans to prosper you and not to harm you, plans to give you hope and a future." This verse reminded me that my purpose isn't found in the world's definition of success but in aligning my life with God's will. Understanding this shattered the illusion of self-reliance and opened my heart to trusting in His greater plan.

4. Faith is a relationship and not a ritual: I grew up believing that faith was about rituals—attending church, reading the Bible, and saying prayers. While these practices are important, they feel hollow without a deeper connection. For years, I went through the motions, thinking that was enough. The turning point came during a moment of worship when I was asked, "Is this how you would serve a King?" It forced me to change my approach to faith. I realized that God desires a relationship, not a checklist. This understanding shattered the illusion of a transactional faith and brought me into a deeper, more personal connection with Him.

5. Truth brings complete freedom: The world offers many illusions of freedom—freedom to choose and to live without restrictions. But these promises often lead to chains: addiction, discontentment, and a sense of purposelessness. When I encountered John 8:32, "Then you will know the truth, and the truth will set you free," it was like a light breaking through the darkness. True freedom isn't found in the absence of boundaries but in living according to God's truth. This

realization shattered the illusion that I could find fulfillment on my own and showed me that true freedom comes from surrendering my will to Him.

4.2 The Power of Truth, Faith, and Courage

My realizations were products of truths. These realizations dawned on me slowly as I gradually discovered the truth. Although my journey to discovering these truths wasn't easy, it was well worth the effort. As the illusions were shattered, I knew that the limitations, chains, and yokes of restrictions that held me were broken. I felt lighter, and freer, and developed a stronger connection and bond with my creator.

However, it wasn't just the knowledge of the truth that brought me freedom. Faith and courage were also necessary. These three were the pillars that supported me on my journey to a life of purpose, freedom, and spiritual fulfillment. All three are necessary forces that guide us through challenges and help us to align with the will of God for our lives. We must take a look at these in greater detail.

1. Truth (the Foundation for Freedom): as earlier established, without the knowledge of the truth, we are vulnerable to the deceptions and illusions of the enemy. In the absence of the truth, we would be led astray by lies. This is why it is an important factor in living a meaningful life. Knowing the truth remains the only way to be free from the bondage that comes with lies and falsehood.
2. Faith (Trusting in the Unseen): the Bible describes faith as the substance of things hoped for and the evidence of unseen realities. Faith not only requires hope but also trust. One of the reasons why it is often difficult to have faith is because doubts and fears constantly surround us. In the face of these doubts, we might find ourselves questioning God rather than trusting Him. However, over the years, faith has taught me the power of absolute surrender to God.
3. Courage (Acting despite Fear): courage is a required factor if we are to act on the truth by faith. Courage is not the absence of fear rather it is the willingness and ability to move forward despite it. Throughout my journey, there were moments when fear threatened

25

to paralyze me—fear of failure, fear of rejection, and fear of stepping into the unknown. These fears were powerful, but they were not greater than the strength God provides. We get to understand the importance of courage when we read the book of Joshua. God promised to be with him and assured him of victory yet he needed to be courageous along the way. Fear loses its grip on us the moment we decide to act courageously.

We need to understand that faith, truth, and courage are interconnected. While truth gives us a foundation to build on, faith encourages us to trust in God's promises while courage propels us to act and take the necessary steps.

We can build our lives on these three powerful forces. Amidst the challenges of life, we can successfully navigate the way out by engaging these powerful principles. These pillars have transformed my perspective, turning doubt into trust, fear into action, and uncertainty into peace. They remind me daily that I am not alone, that God's truth will always prevail, and that with His strength, I can face whatever lies ahead.

4.3 The Holy Bible: The Pathway to True Freedom

The Bible contains the truth that leads us to the path of freedom. This is why we need to embrace the truth of the scriptures with open hearts and minds. To many believers, it is simply a mere historic document or book that is relevant only on Sunday mornings. This was my perspective and view of the scriptures for several years. However, when I changed my approach to the Bible and decided to study it with an open and receptive heart, I found it to be a reliable guide.

Years before I understood the truths of the scriptures, I was immersed in a deep struggle. Much of my internal struggle was a result of the fears and insecurities within me. I felt trapped with what seemed like an invisible chain holding me down emotionally and spiritually. I knew that I needed a guide to help me discover true freedom and peace and I found the Bible to be a reliable one.

The Bible became my guide daily. Through it, I found the answer to several mind-boggling questions. Through God's Word, I found the way out of challenges that came my way each day. As I studied the Bible, it gradually shaped my thoughts and guided my actions daily. I discovered the scriptures to be more than just a collection of stories. God's Word was intentionally written to meet all of man's needs. And as a result, it speaks to every aspect of our lives, addressing our fears and failures.

Through my daily study of the Bible, I understood the following principles that led to my freedom;

1. My Identity in Christ: we cannot learn our true identity as long as we keep listening to the opinions of the world. The world cannot define us because it did not create us. Through the Bible, I learned that I am a beloved child of God created in His wonderful image and glorious likeness. I am defined by who God says I am and not by my mistakes or past failures. A discovery of my identity in the Bible filled me with so much joy and confidence.

2. Trust in the promises of God: developing faith and trust in God took a long time for me. However, as I delved deeper into the scriptures, I was filled with the assurance that God is in control and He is reliable and trustworthy.

3. Freedom through forgiveness: Having previously lived in guilt, bitterness, negativity, and self-condemnation for several years, finding the Bible's teachings on forgiveness was a huge relief to me. It helped me get rid of my guilt and bitterness and experience true freedom instead.

4. Living with purpose: the scriptures opened my eyes to see purpose beyond worldly assumptions. Studying the Great Commission also opened my mind and heart to see that true fulfillment is about living out God's will for our lives and nothing else.

Chapter Five

Living in the Light of Scriptural Truths

The Word of God is the light that shines in darkness. There is no doubt that the entire world is in a state of spiritual darkness. The Bible tells us: "For behold, the darkness shall cover the earth, And deep darkness the people…" (Isa. 60:2). However, amid the darkness that surrounds the world, we can walk in the light. This is one of the reasons why the scriptures were given to us; so that we can live in the light of its truth daily.

The scripture is our only source of light in this world that is filled with so much darkness. The Psalmist realized this when he said: "Your word is a lamp to my feet. And a light to my path." (Ps. 119:105). It is only through the light of scriptures that we can differentiate between right and wrong. This is why it is important to have our character, behavior, choices, and decisions influenced and governed by scriptural truths.

Refusal to live in the light of the truth would mean that we have chosen to walk in the darkness of ignorance, guilt, shame, and self-condemnation. We need to be intentional about our desire to walk in the light of scriptural light in every facet of our lives daily. Walking in the light of scriptural truth also means obedience to every scriptural revelation.

5.1 Birthing Mental Transformation through Scriptural Truths

One of the purposes of the scriptures is to bring about a mental transformation in us. This is to enable us to align our thoughts with the mind of Christ. According to the scriptures, a believer can be carnally or spiritually minded. As a matter of fact, the Bible tells us; "For to be carnally minded is death, but to be spiritually minded is life and peace." (Rom. 8:6). A mental transformation in this context is a change in mindset that is attained when a believer no longer thinks carnally but has become spiritually minded.

Mental transformation is a gradual process and could sometimes take several years of meditating on scriptures before the desired results are achieved. It takes time to shed old beliefs and embrace the truth of the scriptures. It is never easy to create a mental shift. This is because we have been programmed by our old way of thinking and making a change won't come easy.

God's desire is that we become spiritually minded because we cannot please Him as long as we remain carnally minded. Those who are carnally-minded only focus on the pursuit of earthly vanities and material possessions. However, when we are spiritually minded our aim would be on eternal realities and the accomplishment of our divine purpose here on earth.

Mental transformation is a product of our choices and decisions. We have to be intentional because it is not going to happen accidentally. A time comes in our lives when we get fed up with the world's ways of thinking and we desperately need a mental shift.

For several years, my mindset was shaped by the values of the world—success was measured by achievements, self-worth was tied to others' opinions, and happiness depended on circumstances. These beliefs left me feeling restless and unfulfilled, chasing goals that provided only temporary satisfaction.

The turning point came when I began to immerse myself in God's Word. Scriptures such as Romans 12:2 spoke directly to my heart: "Do not conform to the pattern of this world but be transformed by the renewing of your mind." This verse reminded me that true transformation starts with a change in how I think. When we are transformed, we would begin to see life through God's perspective rather than the world's.

Gradually, I replaced worldly values with spiritual truths. I began to understand that my worth is found in being a child of God, not in my accomplishments. I learned to trust in His plan, even when life didn't make sense. I soon began to find joy in His presence rather than in fleeting pleasures. This shift in mindset gave me clarity, focus, and a deep sense of peace.

5.2 How Mental Transformation leads to Changes in Lifestyle

It is a well-known fact that our lives are often a reflection of our minds. It is our thoughts and mindset that determine our attitude and behavior. It is often impossible to separate the thoughts in our minds from the events of our lives. This shows us just how important the state of our mind is.

Changes in our lifestyle therefore begin with intentional changes in our thought patterns. Our mental transformation can only be said to be complete when it is reflected in our lifestyle. When our minds are renewed by the Word of God, our transformation will be obvious to everyone around us.

My journey of transformation wasn't easy. However, as I renewed my mind, I began to notice the following gradual changes in my life daily.

1. Prioritizing spiritual progress: As my mind became renewed, I began to pay more attention to my spiritual growth, progress, and development. Prioritizing my spiritual development means I intentionally had to make time for prayer, Bible study, and fellowship.
2. Aligning actions with values: One of the things I noticed as I renewed my mind was how easy it was for me to align my actions and activities with my core values. I evaluated everything; how I spent my time, the goals I pursued as well as the relationship I nurtured. I intentionally focused on the things that mattered.
3. Letting go of harmful habits: Another thing that was quite easy for me was letting go of harmful habits I had previously struggled with.

It was quite easy to lay aside my negative thoughts and other mundane things that distracted me from focusing on God.

4. Embracing gratitude and contentment: one of the most remarkable changes that came with a renewed mind was a change in my attitude towards gratitude and contentment. Having a renewed mind made me grateful for little things. I also found it easy to choose contentment over comparison. And this filled me with a sense of peace and joy.

While listing the benefits of mental transformation, it is also important to state that the process of transformation is one that requires a great deal of patience because old habits and mindsets won't just disappear overnight. Most often, the process of transformation could take several years before changes become noticeable. Often times, we are tempted to throw in the towel out of frustration because the process seems slow. We need to be determined to stick with the process until our progress becomes evident.

5.3 Viewing Life from a Spiritual Perspective

When we are spiritually minded, it becomes easy to see life from a spiritual perspective. Perhaps the reason some believers are full of worldly ideologies is because they have adopted a carnal approach to life.

For much of my life, I relied solely on what I could see, hear, and understand through a physical and worldly lens. I judged circumstances by their immediate appearance, people by their outward actions, and success by tangible outcomes. However, as I grew in my faith, I began to realize that the world seen through physical eyes is only part of the story. True clarity and understanding come when we learn to see with our spiritual eyes.

Every believer needs to learn to see with their spiritual eyes because relying on our physical eyes alone will limit us. When we view life only from a physical standpoint, we are only focused on the flaws of others as well as the conflicts and obstacles around us. This would hinder us from seeing opportunities for healing, growth, and progress that surround us daily. Relying solely on our physical would only lead to frustration.

31

It is for the purpose of seeing life from a spiritual perspective that God gave us the gift and ability of spiritual sight. All through the scriptures, we are encouraged to develop a spiritual approach to life. This is why the Bible admonishes us to walk with the eyes of faith instead of our physical eyes (2 Cor. 5:7).

Even though the gift of spiritual sight belongs to us, we have to make it a habit to always see things from a spiritual perspective. We can achieve this through the following ways:

1. Relying on scripture: the Word of God is the lens through which we can easily see spiritual realities. The more of the scriptures that we learn about, the more our spiritual capacity is increased.
2. Prayer: all our spiritual potentials are enhanced on the altar of prayer. When we pray, God opens our eyes to see people, things, and situations from a spiritual standpoint.
3. Recognizing spiritual realities: this is one of the ways through which we can learn to see things from a spiritual perspective. By practicing the use of our spiritual sight, we can learn to recognize and discern invisible battles around us. This is very important because our battles are not fought against flesh and blood but against spiritual oppositions.

Learning to see things from a spiritual perspective would definitely impact our lives positively. When we develop a spiritual perspective and approach to life, it becomes easy to see disappointments as blessings and failure as opportunities for growth. We can laugh in the face of adversity because we know it will only work for our good. This was the attitude of Joseph that made him unfazed by the repulsive actions of his brothers who sold him into slavery.

Learning to see with spiritual eyes is an ongoing activity. There are still moments when I fall back into old patterns of focusing only on what is visible. But each time, God gently reminds me to look deeper, to trust Him, and to seek His perspective.

This pattern of viewing things has transformed not only how I see the world but also how I live within it. With spiritual eyes, I can face life's challenges with hope, love others with compassion, and walk confidently in the path God has set before me. It's a gift I am continually grateful for and one that I strive to share with others as I encourage them to see the world through His eyes.

5.4 A New Understanding of Love, Forgiveness, and Purpose

Walking in the light of scriptural truth and developing a spiritual perspective on life would birth a new understanding of certain concepts that were previously unclear to us. For example, there was a time in my life when I thought I understood the meaning of love, forgiveness, and purpose. These concepts seemed straightforward—love was about affection and loyalty, forgiveness was something you granted when necessary, and purpose was tied to goals or accomplishments. However, there were far deeper meanings to these concepts than I ever knew.

I soon realized my understanding of these concepts was at a superficial level. You see, there are varying levels of understanding. When we are carnal, our understanding is quite limited. However, when we observe life from a spiritual perspective, we get a completely different picture.

1. A new understanding of love: My understanding of love had always been from a worldly point of view. Love to me was nothing more than a mere transaction; I only loved those who showed me love. So, I demonstrated love to others based on that condition. However, a new understanding of love from a scriptural point of view soon changed my perspective. I saw God's love to be unconditional. The scripture tells us: "But God demonstrates his own love for us in this: While we were still sinners, Christ died for us" (Rom. 5:8). It dawned on me that if God loved me unconditionally, then my love for others ought not to be conditional. This forever shaped my understanding of the concept of love and I had to learn to love others with patience, kindness, and other biblical attributes of true love.

33

2. A new understanding of forgiveness: The concept of forgiveness has always been a difficult one for people who view life from a worldly point of view. Forgiveness is often viewed as a sign of weakness, so in an attempt to display strength, we intentionally hold on to grudges and bitterness, thereby creating a poison in our hearts. However, the Word of God gave me new insights into the concept of forgiveness. The whole idea of forgiveness is not about excusing the wrongdoings of others but releasing their hold on us. It is an act of grace, modeled after God's forgiveness made available to us through Christ. This understanding made it easy for me to forgive myself and others knowing that God's mercy is greater than our mistakes.

3. A new understanding of purpose: as earlier stated, my understanding of purpose had always been shallow. For me, it had always been about the acquisition of material possessions and worldly success. However, developing a spiritual perspective gave me fresh insight that purpose is about serving God and being a blessing to humanity. It is about fulfilling the higher calling of God upon our lives.

With this new understanding of love, forgiveness, and purpose, my life began to change. Relationships grew deeper as I loved others selflessly and forgave freely. My days felt more meaningful as I pursued a purpose rooted in serving God. With my spiritual eyes now opened, my new understanding of these concepts has made it easy for me to live each day with a new sense of purpose.

Chapter Six

Sharing the Truth with Others

It is not enough to walk in the light of the truth—we need to also bring others into the light by sharing the truth with them. We need to understand that we have been saved, healed, and delivered so we can reach out to others with the same message of salvation, healing, and deliverance. The Bible refers to believers as the light of the world because God has entrusted us with the responsibility of taking the light of the gospel to the ends of the earth.

The only way to liberate our families and friends from the bondage and captivity of the enemy is by sharing the truth with them. Perhaps this is why the enemy is trying to deter us from doing this. Many out there need to hear the message of freedom. Even among believers, many have yet to grasp the revelation of God's love for them.

One of the ways that we can demonstrate our love for God and others is by sharing the message of His love with them. Sometimes the reason we do not get the right response on the mission field is because we are sharing the wrong message. We need to understand that it is the message of God's love that leads to genuine transformation in others. Sharing a message of condemnation and judgment would only lead to guilt and self-condemnation.

6.1 Awakening Others to the Reality of Life

There is no denying the fact that sharing the truth with others could sometimes feel like an uphill task. Awakening others to the reality of life is a deeply personal and spiritual endeavor. However, what is even more

35

important is the approach with which we go about it. We must never attempt to compel others to accept the truth simply because it has transformed us. We need to be patient as we gently admonish others with the truth. We need to understand that by sharing the truth, we have planted seeds. However, we need to patiently trust God as we await the harvest.

I would like to share some tips that I found to be effective when sharing the truth with others.

1. Live by example: Perhaps one of the reasons some people are not successful in their attempt to share the truth with others is that they do not live by example. We need to understand that preaching what we do not practice only makes us hypocrites. There is an old saying that action speaks louder than words. People will only be interested in our message when they see the positive impact that it has had on us. We do not have to be perfect to live by example, neither does living by example mean that we are perfect. However, people can tell when we are honest and sincere or just being hypocritical and phony. I have always made it my aim to be transparent about my struggles while sharing my story with others. I know that I am not superhuman and I am aware of my weaknesses and limitations. However, even in challenging times and circumstances, I always endeavor to reflect on the transformation that God has brought to my heart. This way, I can effectively lead others to the light of the truth that has changed me.

2. Listen to understand: We must learn to listen to others and understand where they are coming from. This way, we can determine the best approach to sharing the truth with them. Everyone has their struggles, questions, and perspectives about life which oftentimes are shaped by past experiences. We need to listen to them as this will help us to understand their perspective, struggles, and questions. Listening builds trust and shows that you genuinely care. It also opens the door for meaningful conversations where you can gently share your own experiences and insights. When people feel heard, they are more open to hearing what you have to share.

3. Share your story: There is no better way to relate with others than to share your personal story. You see, people get encouraged when they

listen to the testimony of how God has helped them to overcome the same challenges that they are going through. Share your story as it is, including the doubts, failures, struggles, and mistakes as well as the turning points that led you to the truth. People can tell the difference between a myth and a true story so be honest as you share.

4. Point them to the source: this perhaps is one of the best ways to help others. As important as it is to share our personal stories. We need to understand that it is not all about us. We need to point people away from us to God who is the source. The easiest way to get people saved and healed is to point them to Jesus the savior and healer. We need to encourage them to develop an intimate relationship with God the Father by praying always and reading the Bible often. We could also give them spiritual resources such as sermons, devotionals, and books that will help them grow spiritually. It is also important that we encourage them to join a local assembly or small spiritual group.

5. Be patient and gracious: It takes time for people to realize the truth. I know this from my personal experience. This is why we need to be patient as we share the truth of God's Word with others. Some might reject the message at first but would later come to light of the truth. We also have to be gracious to those who reject or criticize the message that we share.

6. Pray about it: All our efforts to awaken others to the truth would only lead to nothing unless we commit them to God in prayer. We can do nothing by our strength. The Bible tells us: "Unless the LORD builds the house, they labor in vain who build it; Unless the LORD guards the city,
The watchman stays awake in vain" (Psalms 127:1). We cannot win others through arguments or high-sounding grammar but by the power of God. Through prayer, we can melt even the hardest of hearts.

7. Encourage them to ask questions: Aside from listening to others with whom we share, we should also be willing to entertain their questions and provide answers to them. Providing accurate answers to their questions helps to dissolve their doubts and settle all forms of curiosity.

37

In all that we do, all our actions should be motivated by love. As the old saying goes: "People do not care how much you know until they know how much you care." People will always be willing to listen to us when they sense that we love and genuinely care about them.

6.2 Coping with Rejection, Skepticism, and Dealing with Resistance

One of the challenges we are bound to face as we attempt to awaken others to the truth is resistance, rejection, and skepticism. Many people find it hard to deal with these three negative forces. We need to understand that it is almost impossible for everyone to accept the message that share. When we look closely at the life and ministry of Jesus, we will see that he suffered rejection from his people in Nazareth. He also suffered resistance from the Pharisees, Sadducees, and teachers of the law. Despite the fact that rejection and resistance are inevitable, we should never let them stop us.

We need to understand the root of rejection, skepticism, and resistance. These reactions are often a result of certain factors which include:

1. Fear of change: so often, people react by showing resistance and rejection because they are afraid of the impact that a change of ways might have on them. Hence, they would rather choose resistance and rejection to reformation.
2. Cultural or personal biases: some people are naturally against new ideas and teachings. They generally oppose anything that they are not used to or contrary to their cultural beliefs. Oftentimes, this is a result of the fact that have been deeply ingrained with those beliefs and this makes them resistant to anything that doesn't align with their doctrines or ideologies.
3. Negative experiences: some people have had some negative experiences with some religions in the past. This has created a

level of distrust or resistance to the truth even when it is being shared sincerely.

How to Respond to Rejection

Rejection is no big deal. However, it often comes as a surprise when are rejected by those we least expected. We need to realize that when we are rejected it really isn't about us even though it could sometimes feel personal. Most often when people reject us, it is usually because they do not want to receive the message that we present or the One that we represent.

Jesus was loved by his own people. However, the moment he began to preach the message of repentance, he was rejected by the same people (Jh. 1:11). Since rejection is inevitable it is important that we learn to respond the right way. Even in the face of rejection, we must never respond negatively but continue to show love and support to those who rejected us. It is also important we learn to trust God's plans amidst men's rejection. We must continue to pray for those who rejected us that their eyes would be opened to see the truth about the message that we bring to them.

Navigating Skepticism

Skeptics are usually difficult to deal with because most often, they are full of questions that require a lot of patience to answer. Although skepticism feels like a challenge, it usually opens the door to conversations. To effectively navigate skepticism, we should respect their opinions and be willing to entertain their questions. Most importantly, we need to point them to God and encourage them to develop a personal relationship with Him.

Dealing with Resistance

Much like rejection and skepticism, resistance is inevitable when trying to share with others. We need to deal wisely with resistance because it could come in different forms. We must never deal with resistance with a confrontational approach rather. We need to adopt a peaceful approach. It is also important to avoid further escalation of resistance. We need to know when to back off and just let it go. Even when resistance begins as an argument, we need to respond gently to prevent an escalation. This is why the scripture tells us, "A soft answer turns away wrath, but a harsh word stirs up anger" (Prov. 15:1).

Rejection, skepticism, and resistance are not the end of the world and should not be seen as failure but rather as avenues for growth. We must never let them discourage us.

6.3 Practical Advice for Standing Firm in the Truth

There is a need for us to stand firm in the truth and our faith. The enemy often attempts to frighten us into giving up on what we know and believe in. One of the ways through which he does this is by trying to knock us down with the "strong winds" of wrong doctrine. This is why the scripture admonishes us; "Therefore take up the whole armor of God, that you may be able to withstand in the evil day, and having done all, to stand" (Eph. 6:13). There are days and times when all that we have shared and believed in will be tested. There is a need for us to stand strong so that we can overcome the test. The following tips will help us to stand firmly in the truth:

1. Be firmly rooted in the word of God to be unmovable by negative events and circumstances around you. We can be grounded and rooted in the Word through meditation. As long as we are immersed in the truth of God's Word, we cannot be brought down by the "strong winds" of false doctrine.
2. Praying consistently will help you keep in constant touch with God who is the source of all strength. Prayer has to become our daily habit. Through prayer, we can also discern between truth and falsehood.
3. Endeavor to keep the right company that can give support, strength, inspiration, as well as accountability when needed.
4. Never cower in the face of critics, persecution, or challenging times. Rather let it be an opportunity for growth and self-development.

40

5. Be courageous and bold to preach the truth and live for it each day.
6. Be willing and humble enough to accept corrections.
7. Rely on God and never trust in your strength.

Chapter Seven

Triumphing Over the Enemy Daily

We can have victory over the enemy daily. This is the will of God for us. God has given us all that we need to live triumphantly in this world. We have the light of God that can dispel the enemy's darkness. There is no reason in the world why a believer should be afraid of the vices of the enemy. We cannot be defeated unless we give in to fear and intimidation. Triumphing over the enemy requires boldness and courage.

7.1 The Weapons of our Protection and Warfare: Prayer, Scripture, and Community Fellowship

Our warfare is essentially a spiritual one and requires both spiritual weapons and approach to triumph. The weapons of our warfare are not only useful for launching counterattacks against the enemy, but also for our protection and defense. In a world filled with challenges, distractions, and spiritual battles, protection for the soul is as vital as protection for the body. This is why the Bible admonishes us to put on the whole armor of God.

Despising the weapons of our warfare and defense is the reason why many believers are vulnerable to the attack of the enemy. It is important that we analyze the weapons that guarantees our victory in these end-time battles.

1. Prayer: This is the foundation of our spiritual defense and protection. As a matter of fact, it is the first line of defense for the believer. A prayerless Christian is defenseless and vulnerable to the enemy's attack. Unfortunately, many believers often see prayer as nothing more than a mere ritual or routine. It is only through prayer that we can overcome temptation. This is why the Bible says; "Watch and pray, lest you enter into temptation. The spirit indeed is willing, but the flesh is weak"' (Matt. 26:41). Prayer puts us in a state of spiritual alertness and vigilance. Through prayer, we can overcome spiritual

slumber which is often the reason why we fall into temptation in the first place. Prayer also builds a protective edge around the believer.

2. The Sword of the Spirit: Another weapon of protection available to us is the Word of God which is also referred to as the "Sword of the Spirit" in Ephesians 6:17. The Word of God is the Sword of the Spirit through which we can rightly divide the Word of Truth as instructed in 2 Timothy 2:15. This is what makes it a highly effective weapon against the lies and deception of the enemy. As long as we can rightly divide the Word of truth effectively with the sword of the spirit, we cannot be victims of deception and lies. We need to meditate on scriptures, memorize them, and confess them as often as possible so that they can shield us from the attacks of the enemy.

3. Community Fellowship: When we are amid other believers, we are protected by their community of fellowship. Believers who despise the fellowship of the brethren have made themselves vulnerable to the enemy's schemes. When we are surrounded by the right community of believers then we cannot go wrong.

7.2 Effectively Using the Weapons

To effectively put these weapons to work, we need to use them together so that they can have a synergistic effect. Prayer, scripture, and community fellowship are most effective when combined. In other words, we cannot get the job done by praying, or using the scriptures alone, we need all three. Prayer connects us to God's power, scripture grounds us in His truth, and community strengthens us through fellowship. Together, these three weapons create a holistic defense, equipping us to face life's challenges with confidence and peace.

For example, during a difficult season, prayer can bring immediate comfort and guidance, scripture can offer clarity and reassurance, and the community can provide tangible support and encouragement. By integrating these tools into our daily lives, we build a spiritual foundation that can withstand even the toughest trials.

7.3 Recognizing and Resisting Ongoing Deception

Deception is not always the same, it always presents itself in different patterns and forms. This is why it is often difficult to discern and resist. Every generation will face deception in different forms. Sometimes deception appears in the form of false doctrines. In the Garden of Eden, deception appeared in a form that was difficult for Adam and Eve to recognize and resist.

Deception is so subtle that it can creep into our lives unnoticed in the form of false beliefs, distractions, or even harmless habits. Recognizing deception is evidence of spiritual growth. Learning to recognize distractions involves the following steps:

1. Discern the source: Three major sources exist on the earth: God, man, and Satan. Of these three, only God can be relied on to be pure, true, and void of deception. Both man and Satan are capable of carrying out deception. To recognize deception, we need to discern the source of a thing. Anything that cannot to traced to God's Word either originated from Satan or man and should never be accepted as true. Opinions or views that are not scriptural or that are contradictory to scriptural views are either lies or deception. When evaluating the source of anything, we need to ask ourselves: "Does this align with the Word of God? Is it consistent with His character?"

2. Evaluate the fruit: Not only do we need to examine the source, but we also have to examine the fruit or outcome of anything. We can recognize deception by its fruits of fear, negativity, sin, and others. For instance, when Adam and Eve ate the fruit from the Tree of Knowledge of Good and Evil the consequence was disobedience which led to their expulsion from the Garden of Eden.

3. Discern whether it brings inner peace or unrest: One of the ways through which we can recognize deception is by the absence of inner peace. Anything that originates from God often leads to inner peace. This is why the Psalmist says: "I will hear what God the LORD will speak, For He w speak peace" (Ps. 85:8). Deception on the other hand brings confusion and unrest.

Recognizing deception is important. However, it is not enough to recognize it, we need to be able to resist it in the various forms through which it comes. Here are some of the ways we can resist deception:

1. Guard your heart and mind: The scripture tells us, "Keep your heart with all diligence,
   For out of it spring the issues of life" (Prov. 4:23). It tells us further, "Therefore gird up the loins of your mind..." (1 Pet. 1:13). Our hearts and minds are very important because they are the responsible for receiving and processing the information that we receive. We need to guard them by constantly meditating on the Word of God. When our hearts and minds are filled with the Word of God resisting deception becomes easy.

2. Stand firm in the faith: To resist anything, we must be prepared to stand our ground on what we believe to be right. If we must resist deception, we have to stand firm and be determined never to bow or compromise.

3. Embrace accountability: The whole idea behind accountability is to surround yourself with people who will help you identify the areas where deception might have crept into your life. This will help you retrace your steps and stop deception from building a stronghold in your life.

Chapter Eight

Putting the Truth to Work

The entire essence of learning is application. The reason why we need to learn to resist the lies and deception of the enemy is so that we can put the truth to work. The truth is only powerful when we put it to work. The truth only works when we put it to work. All that you have learned in this book will only work as you put them to work.

We have to engage the truth if we desire to see results. God has revealed the truth to us through His son Jesus Christ, it is now entirely left to us to engage the revealed truth. However, the first step to putting the truth to work is embracing it. We can only engage the truth that we have embraced. The world constantly tries to discourage us from embracing the truth by giving us a distorted view of it. When we courageously engage the truth and put it to work, we will discover that the truth works.

8:1 The Difference Between Knowing and Doing

We have to be intentional about putting the truth to work. It is rather unfortunate that we have a generation of believers who know so much but are doing so little. We need to understand that knowledge is only power when translated into action. The one who knows the truth and does not apply it is no different from the ignorant one.

Knowing the truth ought to be the first step to freedom but for many, it seems to be the only step. Many believers are only content with the knowledge of the truth and are not willing to commit to its application. This has led to accumulated knowledge with little or no results. There's no point in accumulating a bunch of knowledge that will not be applied.

Our daily actions ought to reflect the truth that we have acquired. The only way to prove that we have acquired knowledge is by acting out what we know to be true. Hypocrisy begins when we know the truth enough

46

to share it with others but somehow, we have refused to put it to work in our lives. The Pharisees and Sadducees knew the Law of Moses and even tried to enforce it on others without practicing it themselves.

As believers, we need to understand that it is far easier to witness to others through our actions and lifestyles than preaching a sermon. The difference, therefore, between knowing and doing is the action that we are willing to take.

8:2 The Biblical Admonition on Hearing and Doing

To avoid falling into the trap of knowing and not doing, the Bible admonishes us to act immediately when we hear the truth. James the Apostle wrote:

> [22] But be doers of the word, and not hearers only, deceiving
>
> yourselves.
>
> [23] For if anyone is a hearer of the word and not a doer, he is like a man
>
> observing his natural face in a mirror; [24] for he observes himself, goes away,
>
> and immediately forgets what kind of man he was (Jam. 1:22-24).

When we know the truth and do not practice it, we are in danger of falling into a state of self-deception which is far worse than the enemy's deception. This is why the scripture urges us to act immediately lest we forget to practice what we have heard.

It is rather unfortunate to say that many believers are in a state of self-deception and delusion. Week after week, they hear the Word of God in church and other Christian gatherings but make no effort to put them to work.

47

One of the ways through which the enemy hinders believers from living out the truth is by stealing the Word from their hearts the very instant they hear it. This is because it doesn't matter whether or not folks heard the Word as long as they do not get a chance to practice it, then it won't make much of a difference in their life. Jesus gave an instance of this in the parable of the Sower when he said; "...And these are the ones by the wayside where the word is sown. When they hear, Satan comes immediately and takes away the word that was sown in their hearts" (Mk. 4:15).

Another reason some believers struggle to put the truth to work can be found in Mark 4:19 which tells us: "And the cares of this world, the deceitfulness of riches, and the desires for other things entering in choke the word, and it becomes unfruitful" (Mk. 4:19). You see, the distractions of this world and the pursuit of vain riches can hinder us from putting the truth to work if we do nothing to resist them.

8:3 Encouragement to Embrace the Truth and Live Intentionally

We need to embrace the truth and live intentionally despite the numerous distractions in the world. Life offers us countless opportunities to live meaningfully. Each day presents us with a chance to live a purposeful and positive life. Choosing to live intentionally means evaluating what truly counts, and what does not, and deliberately deciding to focus on what counts.

We need to embrace the truth because it is powerful, timeless, and unchanging. The truth is so powerful that the scripture tells us, "For we can do nothing against the truth, but for the truth" (2 Corin. 13:8). Rejecting the truth does not diminish it, rather it is only to our detriment. We cannot destroy the truth instead we get hurt when we refuse to live by it.

We can live intentionally with the truth daily in the following ways;

1. Define what truly matters: This is the first step to living intentionally with the truth. We have to identify what to focus on and what to ignore.

48

2. Align your actions with the truth: Be deliberate about your actions. Have nothing to do with anything contrary to the truth. Let all your daily actions be consistent with the truth of God's Word.

3. Be determined to learn and grow in the truth: growth is never an easy process. It requires a great deal of determination to keep learning and growing in the truth. As we embrace the truth, we must keep growing in it daily. The truth is inexhaustible this is why we don't have to rest on our oars in the pursuit of it.

4. Celebrate small victories: We have to constantly encourage ourselves by celebrating small milestones and victories on our way.

Embracing the truth and living in it intentionally each day is quite rewarding. Nothing can be more satisfying than to end each day with the knowledge that we have lived intentionally in the truth. Each time we fail to live by the truth, our conscience deep down within signals to us that we aren't living right. Embracing the truth helps us to live with a pure conscience each day.

Conclusion Hope for the Future

It doesn't matter where you are currently in your spiritual journey, you can decide to embrace the truth and live intentionally henceforth. It is never too late to live the way that God intended for you to live. You can make up your mind to begin today, even right away. You can start by taking baby steps. Perhaps you could start by spending some time in prayer and a little more time studying the Bible.

I am not promising that it is going to be an easy journey or a smooth ride but am convinced that it will be worth every step. The future can sometimes look bleak and uncertain. However, when our lives are built and rooted in faith and the truth, we will not be shaken by whatever comes our way. The Bible tells us, "Now hope does not disappoint..." (Rom. 5:5). Hope gives us the confidence we need to face the future, and as long as we are hopeful, we cannot be disappointed. Hope is not a passive feeling; it is an active trust in God's promises, a commitment to live with purpose, and a belief that the best is yet to come when aligned with His will.

God's promises to us are the source of our hope. We can be hopeful of the future because He is faithful to fulfill every one of His promises to us. God has promised us a brighter future. He says in His Word: "For I know the thoughts that I think toward you, says the LORD, thoughts of peace and not of evil, to give you a future and a hope" (Jer. 29:11).

Building a Life and Future Rooted in Faith

Our lives and future must be rooted in faith. This is the only way to build a great future. We must have faith in God at all times. Even when it seems like all hope is lost, we must retain our faith in the Word of God.

Faith means trusting that God's plans unfold in His perfect timing. While it can be difficult to wait or understand delays, faith reminds us that

His perspective is greater than ours. The Bible tells us: "Behold, I lay in Zion a stone for a foundation, A tried stone, a precious cornerstone, a sure foundation; Whoever believes will not act hastily" (Isa. 28:16). You see when our faith is rooted in God, we do not have to act in a hurry or be worried about time. Rather we trust God's time to be the best because His Word tells us that He makes all things beautiful in His time (Ecc. 3:11). Abraham was called the father of faith but he had to wait for 25 years to receive the promised child.

When our lives are built on faith, we won't struggle to obey God. Obedience is one of the signs that we are living by faith. Again, consider our father Abraham. He was obedient to every instruction that he received from God. Firstly, he obeyed the instructions to leave his father's house. He was also obedient to the instruction to circumcise all the males in his household. However, the climax of his obedience came when he was instructed to sacrifice Isaac his son on Mount. Moriah. Abraham had faith that God could bring the dead back to life so he did not hesitate to obey God's instruction to sacrifice Isaac.

Building a life rooted in faith requires that we be thankful every step of the way. Gratitude strengthens our faith. When we are grateful for the past, it fills us with faith for the future.

Living in the Truth

As much as it is important to be rooted in faith, we also need to be rooted in the truth of God's Word. So much has been said about the truth already. However, we must seek the truth through meditation, keep standing firm against deception, and always allow the truth to be reflected in our actions.

A Future Filled with Purposes

When we are rooted in faith and truth, we are set for a life devoted to the fulfillment of God's purpose. This is because faith and truth are essential qualities that are required for walking with God and fulfilling His purposes here on earth. Everyone who was used by God for special purposes as

51

recorded in the scriptures were men and women of faith and truth. Walking in faith and truth will fill us with confidence and also help us to;

1. Maximize the opportunities that come our way in the future: when we walk with God, living each day by faith and in truth, we can be certain that He will bring opportunities our way and open doors to us. This was the case of Joseph who despite being imprisoned, held on to his faith and continued living in the truth until the day he had an opportunity to stand before Pharoah. Although, God opened the door for Joseph, faith and truth helped him maximize the opportunities that came his way.

2. Stay Resilient: Although we all anticipate a bright future; we also know that there are bound to be challenges ahead. However, we can be filled with hope and resilience when we go through tough times because we have faith in God and we know that His promises are true.

3. Invest in others: It becomes easy to share our newfound hope with others when are optimistic about the future. This way we can offer encouragement and support to those around us.

Building a life rooted in faith and truth doesn't eliminate life's uncertainties, but it provides a solid foundation for facing them with courage and peace. It reminds us that no matter what the future holds, God is with us, guiding and sustaining us every step of the way.

Final Thoughts and Gratitude for the Journey

As I reflect on the journey that has brought me to this moment, I am overwhelmed with gratitude. Life has not been without its struggles, doubts, and challenges, but each step along the way has been a part of a greater plan—one that has shaped, refined, and drawn me closer to the truth of who God is and who He created me to be.

This journey has been a process of discovery, growth, and transformation. It has taught me to see beyond life beyond the surface, embrace the reality of God's love, and walk in faith even when the path ahead seems unclear. Every hardship I faced, each question I wrestled with, and every victory I celebrated was significant in shaping my understanding of life, purpose, and truth.

Lessons from the Journey

One of the greatest lessons I've learned is that life is not about perfection—it's about progress. It's about being willing to seek truth, grow through challenges, and trust God's plan even when it doesn't align with mine. I've learned that setbacks are not the end but an opportunity for new beginnings and that every step forward, no matter how small, brings me closer to the life God has called me to live.

Another invaluable lesson is the power of gratitude. Even in the hardest moments, there has been something to be thankful for—whether it's the support of loved ones, the strength to persevere, or the quiet assurance of God's presence. Gratitude has been a lifeline, reminding me to focus on the blessings rather than the burdens and to see God's hand at work in every situation.

53

A Heart of Gratitude

I am deeply grateful to God for His faithfulness, patience, and unending love. He has been my guide, strength, and refuge throughout this journey. In moments of doubt, He provided clarity. In moments of weakness, He gave me strength. And in times of despair, He reminded me of His promises and purpose for my life.

I am also thankful for those who have walked alongside me—those who encouraged, challenged, and inspired me to keep going. Their love and support have been a reflection of God's grace, and I am forever grateful for their presence in my life.

Lastly, I am thankful for the journey itself. While it hasn't always been easy, it has been worth every step. Each trial has deepened my faith, each question has led to greater understanding, and each moment of surrender has brought me closer to the truth.

Looking Ahead

As I close this chapter of my journey, I am filled with hope for what lies ahead. The lessons I've learned and the truths I've embraced are not just for me—they are meant to be shared to inspire and encourage others to seek their paths of discovery and growth.

The journey is far from over, and I know there will be more challenges to confront and lessons to learn. But I am confident that the same God who has brought me this far will continue to lead, guide, and use me for His glory.

Final Encouragement

To those who read these words, I encourage you to embrace your journey with courage, faith, and an open heart. Seek the truth, live intentionally, and trust that God is with you every step of the way. There is beauty in the process, and purpose in every moment, even the difficult ones.

Thank you for joining me on this journey. It is my prayer that the lessons I've shared will inspire and encourage you as you walk your path, discovering the incredible love, truth, and purpose that God has for you.

About the Author

Georgie A. McKenzie is a devoted follower of Jesus Christ and a dedicated advocate for helping others discover truth and purpose through faith. With a heart for serving God and a passion for sharing life-changing insights, Georgie draws from personal experiences and biblical principles to inspire others to live intentionally and embrace the freedom found in God's love.

Growing up as the youngest of eleven children, Georgie developed a deep sense of introspection and a natural curiosity about life's meaning. Despite attending church from a young age, Georgie's journey of faith took a transformative turn in adulthood when an encounter with a prophetic ministry opened their eyes to the true essence of serving a living God. This pivotal moment ignited a renewed commitment to living in alignment with God's will and sharing the lessons learned along the way.

Through trials, triumphs, and an unwavering reliance on God's grace, Georgie has developed a profound understanding of what it means to walk in truth and overcome the deceptions of the world. Georgie's life is deeply rooted in authenticity, compassion, and a desire to encourage others to seek God's presence and fulfill their unique calling.

About the Book

Clearing the Fog: A Journey to Truth, Faith, and Purpose is a testament to Georgie A. McKenzie's transformative spiritual journey and unwavering dedication to helping others deepen their faith and embrace intentional living. Through life and work, Georgie strives to honor the Lord Jesus Christ, inspiring others to draw closer to Him and discover the freedom and purpose found in His truth.

"To God be all the glory for the life He has given me and the privilege to share His truth with the world."

www.ingramcontent.com/pod-product-compliance
Lightning Source LLC
Chambersburg PA
CBHW070025110426
42741CB00034B/2562